# THE MENTORING POCKETBOOK

D0434088

## By Geof Alred, Bob Garvey & Richard Smith

*Drawings by Phil Hailstone*

"Mentoring is probably the most powerful developmental process people can experience. And when it works, it develops two for the price of one. *The Mentoring Pocketbook* is a no-nonsense primer for the first-time mentor or mentee."
**Prof. David Clutterbuck, Co-founder, The European Mentoring and Coaching Council**

"Whether you are thinking about working with a mentor, becoming a mentor yourself, engaged in a current mentoring relationship, or developing a mentoring approach as part of reshaping your organisation's development agenda, you will find this pocketbook extremely informative. It offers well researched, uncomplicated practical advice and suggestions for mentee and mentor alike – a great resource."
**Kevin Galloway, Leadership Development Manager, Halifax Bank of Scotland**

*Published by:*
**Management Pocketbooks Ltd**
Laurel House, Station Approach, Alresford, Hants SO24 9JH, U.K.
Tel: +44 (0)1962 735573   Fax: +44 (0)1962 733637
E-mail: sales@pocketbook.co.uk
Website: www.pocketbook.co.uk

First published in 1998.  This edition published 2006.  Reprinted 2007, 2008, 2009.

© Geof Alred, Bob Garvey & Richard Smith 1998 and 2006.

ISBN  978 1 903776 353

British Library Cataloguing-in-Publication Data – A catalogue record for this book
is available from the British Library.

Design, typesetting and graphics by **efex ltd.**   Printed in U.K.

# CONTENTS

> "Mentoring is a learning relationship between two people. It requires a range of human qualities such as trust, commitment and emotional engagement. It also involves a range of skills including listening, questioning, challenge and support. Mentoring has a time scale. In some contexts it is a life long relationship, in others it may be a few months."
>
> A mentoring researcher

# HOW TO USE THIS POCKETBOOK

This book is a resource and support for those involved in mentoring at work. It will be useful to anyone who is interested in professional and personal learning. It is aimed mainly at mentors, but mentees and scheme co-ordinators will also find it helpful.
It can be used in a number of ways:

- **As an outline resource book:** it gives you a clear idea of how to design and manage schemes, prepare for mentoring, conduct mentoring sessions, maintain the mentoring relationship and evaluate mentoring

- **For reflection:** it is a resource to consult, particularly when you are approaching a mentoring session or when you want to reflect, after a session, about what has gone on

- **To stimulate your development as a mentor:** the book provides a challenge and stimulus to reflect upon your role within your organisation, and what you value as a member of your organisation

Continued ...

# HOW TO USE THIS POCKETBOOK

- **To stimulate your development as a mentee:** it may help you to develop your career and yourself personally

- **For discussion:** the book can be a focus for discussion with mentees in mentoring sessions and with other mentors in your network; it may also provide a focus for discussion with your line manager

- **To read selectively:** the book is designed to be read in any way which you feel appropriate, either the sections relevant to you or from cover to cover

**Note** Where this book talks of the 'mentee' others sometimes use the words 'protégé', 'mentoree' or 'learner'. 'Mentee' is our preferred term.

# MENTORING
# IN ORGANISATIONS

## MENTORING IN ORGANISATIONS

# WHERE IT IS FOUND

Mentoring is rapidly becoming recognised worldwide as a highly effective human resources development process. Examples can be found in many diverse organisations from public to private sector, from service to manufacturing industries. A recent study in the UK reported that 238,000 people in the National Health Service have had access to mentoring! There are mentoring programmes in:

- Manufacturing industries
- Retail businesses
- Airlines and travel
- Financial services
- Tourism and leisure

- Educational institutions
- Petro-chemical industries
- Public sector and government
- Charities, not for profit and social sector
- The armed and emergency services

# WHY MENTORING & WHY NOW?

Why is mentoring so widespread?

**In organisations, mentoring supports:**

- Knowledge development and knowledge sharing
- The development of effective learning environments
- Value added performance and productivity development
- The changing role of managers – from command and control to challenge and support
- People in changing situations
- Stress management initiatives
- Management, capability, talent and leadership development
- Creativity and innovation
- Problem solving skills development
- Strategic decision making

# WHY MENTORING & WHY NOW?

**In wider society, mentoring within the community, education and health sectors supports:**

- Social integration and change
- Citizenship development
- Educational policies and learning
- Behaviour and attitude change
- New patient care initiatives
- Wider participation and diversity
- Social policy implementation

MENTORING IN ORGANISATIONS

# POSSIBLE USES

Mentoring is used in organisations for various purposes, eg:

- **Induction:** to help people become familiar with the organisation and get up to speed
- **Leadership development:** to help develop leadership abilities
- **Succession planning:** to develop potential managers of the future
- **Talent programmes:** to develop talent, potential and capability
- **Support for development:** to ensure effective learning for the future
- **Career progression:** to assist in identifying and supporting potential
- **Support for learning on the job:** to enhance job-related knowledge and skills
- **Diversity programmes:** to respect, develop, appreciate and understand diversity
- **Redundancy support:** to assist people in new stages of their lives
- **Support in a new project or new job:** to ensure rapid assimilation and delivery
- **Within change programmes:** to help people understand what is involved in change

# DEALING WITH CHANGE

Many organisations have gone through or are currently going through significant change. Change is a constant feature of organisational life. Generally, people in any organisation react positively to change when they take responsibility for their own development.

Organisations recognise this when they write their Mission or Strategic Statements. Good organisations also recognise the importance of the role they play in offering assistance to people during periods of change. Mentoring is one way in which organisations can provide this assistance.

# MISSION STATEMENTS

The idea that people make the difference is often present in mission and strategic statements. For example:

> *"Able and Co. will be a fast moving, customer-focused organisation, ensuring value for money, and getting results through well-motivated staff."*

> *"We recognise the importance of our human assets in delivering our company's mission."*

> *"Jones Ltd's people will be empowered to secure effective and exceptionally responsive service to customers."*

> *"We aim for extraordinary customer satisfaction through a people-focused strategy."*

> *"Our mission will be achieved through the willing efforts of all our people."*

> *"People are the fundamental asset on which the company's success will be based."*

# VALUE STATEMENTS

Many organisations establish a set of values in order to describe how their business should operate.

Values are often written down as part of the organisation's strategy, eg:

- To **delight the customer**, by providing the right advice, right information at the right time
- To be **ethically led**
- To **respect and value people's opinions**, through our diversity policy
- To **focus on people**, by supporting and developing staff
- To **encourage openness in all our business dealings**, through developing a 'blame-free' environment
- To **strive for excellence** in the delivery of all our services
- To deal with all our staff and clients with **fairness and honesty**
- To be viewed as a **'good' employer** in the market place
- To recognise and act on both our **corporate and social responsibilities**

# VALUES

✔ **Mentoring** helps people to understand how a company's values are realised in the organisation. It helps them feel that they are making a worthwhile contribution.

✔ **Mentoring** has strategic development implications. It is consistent with the Investors in People standard and is often supported by the organisation's development and training strategy.

✔ **Mentoring** can make a contribution to the delivery of the Mission and Strategy and the achievement of objectives. It helps to uphold organisational values.

✔ **Mentoring** helps individuals to develop within the organisational framework.

# FROM THE FRONT LINE

> *"Mentoring helps people understand and work through change and so contributes to the achievement of the Mission or Strategy. Mentoring helps people to learn and supports self-development."*
>
> An experienced mentor

# THINKING ABOUT MENTORING

# WHAT IS MENTORING?

In mentoring, the relationship between mentor and mentee is all-important.

- There is a high degree of trust and mutual regard

- The mentor helps the mentee become what that person aspires to be

- The mentee is helped to realise his or her potential

- The mentor learns and develops also, through being a mentor and developing mentoring skills

# WHAT IS MENTORING?

You have probably been mentored already! Many people can remember being helped by someone who took an interest in their welfare, shared their experience and knowledge with them, and enabled them to develop.

Often they remember these relationships as playing a crucial part in their personal and professional development.

# WHAT IS MENTORING?

A good mentor remembered:

*"When I joined the organisation I was asked after a few weeks to find someone to be my mentor. I asked Peter since we worked in the same section and he was friendly and approachable. We set aside an hour a week so I could talk through issues that were concerning me. We ranged over a lot of issues, personal as well as professional. Peter would make sure we finished the meeting with action points that I would try to follow up on, and that would often be where we started from the next week. But I could always ask him questions between our meetings as well. It was valuable to be able to turn to him over the kind of small matters that you would hesitate to bother some people with, especially your line manager. Peter helped me to get a picture of the whole organisation and my place in it. Thanks to him I settled in quickly and built up a sense of how my career might develop and what I needed to learn in order to make progress."*

## THINKING ABOUT MENTORING

# IDENTIFY YOUR OWN MENTORS

Ask yourself the following questions:

- Who took an interest in my welfare and development at a time when I was taking on challenges, such as starting a new job?
- Who has been a useful role model in my life?
- Who helped me to uncover and use a hidden talent or ability?
- Who helped me face and resolve a difficult situation in my personal and/or professional life?
- Who challenged me to acquire a new vision and take a new direction?
- Who supported me to acquire a new vision and take a new direction?

These people have been your mentors.

# FAMOUS MENTORS

There have been many well-known examples of the mentoring relationship throughout history, including:

**In Music**
Haydn and Mozart
Clive Davis and Carlos Santana

**In Sport**
Alex Ferguson and Wayne Rooney
Brian Close and Ian Botham

**In Politics**
Peter Thompson and Tony Blair

**In Ancient Greek History**
Mentor (Athene) and Telemachus

# MENTOR & MANAGER

As a **manager** you are concerned with the objectives of both team and organisation.

As a **mentor** you help your mentee to learn within the context of a supportive relationship.

Mentoring and managing are not completely distinct. Managers may often use mentoring as part of their line role. They also recognise the value of an employee having a separate mentor, as this will enhance the overall performance of the employee and his or her contribution to the team. A skilled manager may work with members of their team using a mentoring style, because he or she recognises that this enhances understanding, co-operation, performance and commitment.

# MENTOR & MANAGER

When the mentor is somebody different from the manager this does not have to be a threat to the manager's authority. The benefits of mentoring to the manager and his or her team will emerge in the form of greater commitment, motivation and learning on the part of the mentee.

It is important that:

- There is as much openness and honesty as possible between the line manager, mentor and mentee
- The confidentiality of the mentoring relationship is respected

# MENTOR & MANAGER

> *"One of the things mentors and mentees should do is to make sure that the mentee's line manager knows that mentoring is going on."*
>
> An experienced service industry mentee

THINKING ABOUT MENTORING

# TYPES OF MENTEE

There is no blueprint for the ideal mentoring relationship. You may be a mentor to:

- A peer
- A team member
- Someone you know well
- Someone you have not met before
- Someone from a different department or function
- Someone from a different organisation

It is usually not advisable to have your line manager as your mentor because at times there may be a conflict of interest. In some circumstances a line manager can be a mentor but care has to be taken in establishing clear ground rules and a mutually agreed agenda.

What is common to all cases of mentoring is that the mentee comes to view things in a new way. The mentor promotes change in the mentee, helping that person towards a new vision of what is possible.

# BENEFITS OF MENTORING

**For the mentee**

- Improved performance and productivity
- Enhanced career opportunity and career advancement
- Improved knowledge and skills development
- Leadership development
- Greater confidence, well-being, commitment and motivation

**For the mentor**

- Improved performance
- Greater job satisfaction, loyalty, commitment and self-awareness
- New knowledge and skills acquired
- Leadership development
- Reduced conflict and improved relationships with colleagues and customers

# BENEFITS OF MENTORING

### For both

- Wider perspectives on the organisation and the market
- Improved strategic thinking
- Extended business networks and enhanced business opportunities

### For the line manager

- A more motivated, effective and resourceful team member
- Improved skills and knowledge in the team
- Improved performance capability and opportunity

### For the organisation

- Improved productivity and performance
- Improved implementation of strategies and policies
- Improved staff retention, morale and motivation
- Improved communication and relationships with colleagues and customers
- Improved knowledge exchange and learning

# MENTORING & COACHING

Mentoring and coaching have much in common. The evidence from current practice suggests that the differences between mentoring and coaching are becoming blurred and the similarities are becoming more apparent.

Coaching takes many different forms, for example, performance coaching, sports coaching and life coaching. Coaching tends to have a specific and tightly focused goal, or area of application.

Mentoring goes further in offering support and advice to someone as a person, and whilst there is usually a focus (eg taking up a new post), mentoring can touch on any aspect of a person's life. The mentor may offer coaching and training from time to time as appropriate, but may also encourage the mentee to seek help from specialists in these roles.

# MENTORING & COACHING

Broadly speaking the differences can be summed up as:

| Mentoring | Coaching |
|---|---|
| Implications beyond task | Task orientation |
| Capability and potential | Skill and performance |
| Best off-line or external | Online, offline or external |
| Agenda with learner | Agenda set with or by coach |
| Reflection by the learner | Reflections to the learner |
| Longer term | Shorter term |
| Feedback intuitive, implicit | Feedback explicit |

(adapted from Megginson, D and Clutterbuck, D (2005) *Techniques for Coaching and Mentoring*,
Elsevier Butterworth-Heinemann, Oxford)

# TYPES OF MENTORING

There are two main types of mentoring – developmental and sponsorship.

*Developmental* mentoring is what it says on the tin! It is aimed at supporting the mentee's learning and development as he or she goes through some sort of change. The change could be learning new skills, acquiring new knowledge, changing behaviours and attitudes, developing awareness of others and self. This type of mentoring is the most widespread across all organisational sectors and other mentoring settings in the UK.

*Sponsorship* mentoring is about fast tracking the mentee in their career. Broadly, this has been the dominant model in the US, whilst more recently developmental mentoring has become more common.

# FROM THE FRONT LINE

> *"I found the literature on mentoring confusing until I realised the term meant something rather different for Americans. For them it's much more a matter of bringing people on in their professional roles as quickly as possible, even of offering opportunities for high-flyers to race up the career ladder."*
>
> A personnel manager in manufacturing industry

# MENTORING & APPRAISAL

Mentoring and appraisal use many of the same techniques.

The difference are:

**Appraisal** is part of a formal system which identifies strengths and weaknesses, and may be linked to performance-related pay, to opportunities for promotion or the requirement to undertake training.

**Mentoring** is not formally connected with structures of extrinsic reward - or penalty! The mentor is non-judgemental, and does not impose his/her views on any third party. The mentee can be candid with the mentor in a way that would be unlikely in the context of appraisal.

NOTES

# THE MENTORING PROCESS

# GETTING STARTED

Although mentoring is a common, often unrecognised, activity, it is a form of helping that most people could develop further. Effective mentoring requires certain personal qualities and skills.

**How will you know that you are ready to be a mentor?**

This is an important question. You can address it in a number of ways:

- Recognise and reflect on any mentoring you do already
- Talk to other mentors
- Talk to people you have already mentored (officially or unofficially)
- Consider the differences between mentoring and management
- Consider the differences between mentoring and other ways of helping, eg: coaching, appraisal, counselling
- Reflect upon your own experience of being a mentee

# THE MENTORING PROCESS

# GETTING STARTED

**How will you know that you are ready to be a mentor?**

You can also address this question by thinking about your attributes using the list below:

- A range of experience and variety of workplace skills
- A good understanding of the organisational context
- A sense of commitment to the organisation, its values and mission
- Good listening skills
- Well-developed interpersonal skills
- An ability to relate well with people who want to learn
- An interest in helping and developing others
- An open mind, a flexible attitude, and a recognition of your own need for support
- Time and willingness to develop relationships with mentees

**Do you have these attributes? If so, you are ready to mentor.**

# GETTING STARTED

> *"I'm now about to become a mentor myself, having attended a mentoring workshop. I don't know if anyone I mentor will be fortunate enough to get as much out of the experience of being mentored as I did. But if I can contribute to someone else's development in some way then, hopefully, the experience will be rewarding both for the mentee and for myself."*
>
> A manager approaching the mentoring role

# AREAS OF DEVELOPMENT

A mentor can help a mentee to:

- Understand appropriate behaviour in social situations
- Understand the workings of the organisation
- Acquire an open flexible attitude to learning
- Understand different and conflicting ideas
- Be aware of organisational politics
- Overcome setbacks and obstacles
- Acquire technical expertise
- Gain knowledge and skills
- Develop personally
- Adjust to change
- Develop values

# THE MENTORING PROCESS

## 3-STAGE MODEL

Mentoring includes a number of processes. Different mentors have different strengths and work in different ways. Whatever approach or style you use, working within a well-thought out, robust and flexible framework will ensure you are most effective in helping your mentee.

A useful framework is a 3-stage model* of helping:

**1** EXPLORATION  **2** NEW UNDERSTANDING  **3** ACTION PLANNING

* Adapted from the 'skilled helper model' described in Gerard Egan's *Skilled Helper: A Problem Management and Opportunity Development Approach to Helping,* 7th Edition, 2002 Brooks/Cole, Pacific Grove, California.

THE MENTORING PROCESS

# 3-STAGE MODEL

The model can be used in a number of ways:

- To **reflect** upon what mentoring involves, and to **assess** yourself as a mentor
- As a **schedule** for a mentoring meeting - to work through the stages
- As a **map** of the mentoring process - to see what ground has been covered and what needs further attention
- To **review** the mentoring relationship over time, as the mentee moves towards achieving the goals identified earlier in the relationship
- To **enhance** shared understanding of the mentoring process and relationship, and to develop the mentee's ability to use the model independently

THE MENTORING PROCESS

# 3-STAGE MODEL

> "Mentoring gives me a real buzz and makes me feel unbelievably good that somebody can learn and develop with my help. It has enabled my influence to spread in the organisation and thus assist the change process in a way which is more powerful than any other process I know."
>
> An NHS manager and mentor

# THE MENTORING PROCESS

## STAGE 1: EXPLORATION

**Strategies**

As mentor, you aim to:
- Take the lead by listening
- Pay attention to the relationship and develop it
- Clarify the aims and objectives of the mentoring
- Support the exploration

**Methods**

As mentor, you:
- Negotiate an agenda
- Listen carefully
- Ask open questions
- Summarise

 **1** EXPLORATION  **2** NEW UNDERSTANDING  **3** ACTION PLANNING

# THE MENTORING PROCESS

## STAGE 1: EXPLORATION
### GETTING MAXIMUM BENEFIT

- Take the lead in creating a **rapport** with your mentee and an atmosphere that encourages exploration; show your **commitment** to the mentee, the mentoring process and the mentoring relationship

- Give it time, **be patient**; action plans come unstuck when rushed, and insufficient exploration leads to faulty understanding in Stage 2 and hence to inappropriate plans (investment of time and care in Stage 1 pays dividends later in the meeting and later in the relationship)

- Help your mentee to arrive at **his or her own answers**

- Resist the temptation to give advice or tell the mentee what to do (there are occasions when advice and direction are helpful, but not in Stage 1)

THE MENTORING PROCESS

# STAGE 1: EXPLORATION
POSSIBLE QUESTIONS/COMMENTS

As a mentor, you might say:

'What would you like to talk about today?'

'What I understand you to be saying is... (paraphrase/summarise). Does that seem right?'

'Let's explore this issue some more.'

'Shall we start by recapping on our last meeting?'

'Tell me about your experience of...'

'You've said very little about X, but that seems to be central to the issue we are discussing.'

THE MENTORING PROCESS

# STAGE 1: EXPLORATION
### HOW LONG DOES STAGE 1 LAST?

This is an important question but it does not have a straightforward answer. It is important to think about how much time to give to exploring an issue so that you can assess progress.

Much depends upon the topic being explored:

 • If it is something **significant**, related to changes in personal or professional attitudes and behaviours, you may find that you need to explore an issue on and off for several months or longer

 • If it is a **practical** topic, related to knowledge or skills, it may take a few minutes or a few hours

Either as mentor or mentee, if you feel that you are stuck in a rut of endless exploration with no progress, it is time to talk about your relationship.

# THE MENTORING PROCESS

## STAGE 2: NEW UNDERSTANDING

**Strategies**

As mentor, you aim to:
- Support and understand
- Be constructive and positive
- Recognise strengths
- Establish priorities
- Identify developmental needs

**Methods**

As mentor, you:
- Listen and challenge
- Ask open and closed questions
- Summarise and clarify
- Give information and advice
- Share experiences and tell stories

# STAGE 2: NEW UNDERSTANDING

## GETTING MAXIMUM BENEFIT

Stage 2 is the **turning point** in the process. New understanding is experienced in a number of ways, depending on the individual and the importance of the issue in hand. Be flexible and resourceful, ready to move forward (and sometimes backwards) empathically and constructively with the mentee.

New understanding often releases energy, it can be exciting. Once your mentee begins to see things differently, offer **encouragement**. Progress can be rapid but again - **don't rush**.

Arriving at a new understanding can be uncomfortable: the mentee may be resistant. Then progress can be slow and erratic. This could signal the need for more exploration.

Be ready to return to Stage 1, eg: 'Now that you appreciate better the impact of working with new colleagues, perhaps you would like to look again at your thoughts about further training'.

# STAGE 2: NEW UNDERSTANDING

## GETTING MAXIMUM BENEFIT (Cont'd)

If the mentee is resistant, be **supportive** and **sensitive** so that when you **challenge**, your mentee is receptive and able to learn.

Challenge **positively**, eg: refer to the mentee's achievements, positive qualities and potential, as well as offer constructive criticism of current behaviour, perceptions and attitudes that may be causing problems. **Be patient.**

New learning can make the mentee feel vulnerable, especially if it requires recognition that old ways of behaving have outlived their usefulness and there is a need to change.

# STAGE 2: NEW UNDERSTANDING

## GETTING MAXIMUM BENEFIT (Cont'd)

Help your mentee **consolidate** his/her learning, to hold on to the fruits of the exploration in Stage 1.  One way to do this is to **share stories** and **experiences** of your own.

Don't share too soon, as new learning can be fragile at first.  There is a risk of taking the mentee away from his/her own agenda.

**Reflect** back and clarify what the mentee has learned and the implications of **new developmental needs, goals and aspirations**.

## STAGE 2: NEW UNDERSTANDING
POSSIBLE QUESTIONS/COMMENTS

As mentor, you might say:

'What are your options here and what might be the consequences of doing X?'

'What is there to learn here, what's the most important thing to work on, now that you're seeing the situation differently?'

'The way you're talking now reminds me of the time I...'

'Well done, that feels like a breakthrough.'

'Now that doing X looks like a viable option, there is some useful information I could share with you.'

'You've shown real commitment in the situation, but there are also things you've done that you regret. Is that a fair comment?'

THE MENTORING PROCESS

# STAGE 2: NEW UNDERSTANDING
## HOW LONG DOES STAGE 2 LAST?

Reaching new understandings is key to the next stage. Action born out of poor understanding is always flawed! This stage should not be rushed, although reaching a new understanding can happen quite spontaneously during a Stage 1 discussion.

 It may take hours, days, weeks, months and even years to fully understand a complex issue.

The timescale is dependent on experience, the nature and complexity of the issue and the quality of the mentoring conversations.

# THE MENTORING PROCESS

## STAGE 3: ACTION PLANNING

### Strategies

As mentor, you aim to:

- Examine options for action and their consequences
- Review the mentoring process and the relationship
- Negotiate an action plan

### Methods

As mentor, you:

- Encourage new and creative ways of thinking
- Help to make decisions and solve problems
- Agree action plans
- Monitor progress and evaluate outcomes
- Coach

1 EXPLORATION 2 NEW UNDERSTANDING **3 ACTION PLANNING**

THE MENTORING PROCESS

# STAGE 3: ACTION PLANNING
## GETTING MAXIMUM BENEFIT

When Stages 1 and 2 are done thoroughly, Stage 3 is usually straightforward and uses familiar **people management/development skills**.

Plans are followed through when the mentee **owns** the solution. Give advice and direction sparingly. Enhance **commitment** to change by clear agreements and target setting.

Look after the **relationship**, discuss its progress with your mentee. **Don't expect every meeting to end in an action plan**. Sometimes the action will be to meet again, and that will be progress enough. Affirm and celebrate progress.

THE MENTORING PROCESS

# STAGE 3: ACTION PLANNING
POSSIBLE QUESTIONS/COMMENTS

As mentor, you might say:

'Let's look at the pros and cons of this option.'

'Let's spend some time talking about the mentoring itself, as we agreed to review after three months. Perhaps we could do it over lunch.'

'How can I help you do this? Perhaps a demonstration of X would help.'

'Now that you've decided to do Y, is there anything you need to do first?'

THE MENTORING PROCESS

# STAGE 3: ACTION PLANNING
## HOW LONG DOES STAGE 3 LAST?

The important point here is that it can be very tempting to rush to action. This is often true when there is a lot of pressure on people to perform at work.

The quality of action is firmly linked to the quality of Stages 1 and 2.

 Sometimes the action phase is immediate but, in the case of complex attitudinal and behavioural issues, it may take weeks, months or even years to fully develop.

Mentoring is seldom about 'quick fixes'. If it is to work really well, a longer-term view is necessary.

# FROM THE FRONT LINE

*"To be a successful mentor enjoy what you're doing as well as BELIEVE in your mentee. Do not hesitate to ask for help from another mentor with special expertise. Friendship and rapport are important. The rewards of being a mentor are similar to the enriching experiences of meeting interesting people and facing the challenges of solving difficult problems. A good mentor, therefore, brings enjoyment of people and ideas and a strong belief to the mentoring situation."*

A mentor with many years' experience

# FACILITATING LEARNING

Another way to look at mentoring is by making use of the learning cycle, based on Kolb's theory of experiential learning. An awareness of the cycle can help the mentor and mentee to focus on the mentee's learning.

Have an experience

Think about the experience

Generalise from the experience

Apply the experience

# THE LEARNING CYCLE

The mentor helps the mentee round the learning cycle by asking questions such as:

'Tell me about your experience of...'

'What do you think this means?'

'What general lessons can be drawn from your understanding?'

'How can you apply this understanding?'

## THE MENTORING PROCESS

# FINDING A MENTEE

In your organisation, your mentee may be somebody you know already. An existing relationship may develop into mentoring.

Your organisation may have a formal mentoring scheme or some system for facilitating mentoring. Then a match will be arranged.

It may be policy in your organisation for employees to be assigned a mentor in certain situations, for instance as part of induction for new employees or when an employee takes on new responsibilities (see section on Scheme Design).

# THE MENTORING PROCESS

## FINDING A MENTOR

If you have identified someone who could be your mentor ask yourself:

- Will this individual stretch and challenge my thinking?
- Is the experience gap between us too small or too great?
- Is this individual willing to learn and develop?
- Would we have mutual respect?

# WHEN MENTEE CHOOSES MENTOR

Mentoring is primarily for the mentee, **for their welfare, development, progress,** within the context of their responsibilities and ambitions within the organisation.
A person seeks a mentor because he or she recognises
the need for mentoring support, or the need is
recognised by a concerned third party
(eg the person's manager).

'could I have your thoughts on.....'

As a mentor, what do you think would be
helpful for your mentee to know about you?
Put yourself in their position.
The information you give about yourself
needs careful thought. It can help to write
it down or talk it through with a trusted friend,
or your own mentor (see section on Scheme Design).

# BEING A MENTOR

Keep in mind that a mentee will benefit from your:

- Knowledge
- Experience
- Personal qualities and skills

# BEING A MENTOR
## KNOWLEDGE

Think about your knowledge of
the **organisation:**

- Its politics
- Its culture
- Its history
- Its character

# BEING A MENTOR

## EXPERIENCE

As a mentor you will draw on your experience of:

- Facing difficulties
- Meeting new challenges
- Being helped, being a mentee
- Working with others, contributing to an organisation
- Achievement, success, failure
- A variety of organisations/working practices
- Being responsible for yourself, your actions and reactions to others and situations
- Trauma and setback
- Coping with stress

# BEING A MENTOR

## PERSONAL QUALITIES

As a mentor you will draw on your ability to be:

- **Enthusiastic** - genuinely interested in the mentee and his/her concerns, needs, dreams and aspirations
- **Motivating and encouraging** - to channel the mentee's energy into constructive change, new challenges and overcoming difficulties
- **Open** - prepared to share your own experience of similar issues, be honest about yourself, be honest about the mentee
- **Empathic** - able to appreciate how the mentee thinks and feels and behaves
- **Positive in your outlook** - able to appreciate the mentee's point of view and see solutions
- **A good listener** - able to really focus on what the mentee is saying without your own thoughts crowding out the mentee's words

# FROM THE FRONT LINE

> *"Fit and chemistry must be considered when pairing the mentor and the protégé. If the two don't get along, it matters little what each can offer the other in terms of knowledge and skills."*
>
> Michael Zey, *Building a successful formal mentor programme*

# THE MENTORING PROCESS

## BEING A MENTEE

People learn how to be a mentee through being part of a mentoring relationship.
With commitment, experience and practice, mentees become better at making the most
of the mentoring process.  Successful mentees:

✔ Accept **challenge** willingly; they are **committed** to the mentoring process

✔ Are prepared to be **open** and **honest** about themselves

✔ Take **responsibility** for their own learning

✔ Have **trust** and **confidence** in their mentor; they are willing to discuss issues openly

✔ Recognise that learning can involve taking **risks** in order to make progress

# BEING A MENTEE

Successful mentees also:

✔ Want to be **active** in their development and see learning as a **continuing process**

✔ Make **progress**, and **recognise** when the relationship is reaching its natural end

When the mentee **owns** the process and **understands** the 3-Stage Model, the quality of learning is improved.

# THE MENTORING PROCESS

## MENTEES' EXPECTATIONS

Mentees who understand the value of mentoring and are committed to a mentoring relationship, expect to gain by:

- Being challenged
- Opening up and being honest
- Learning through discussion
- Learning from example and from mistakes
- Receiving support, feedback and advice
- Listening and being listened to
- Becoming more self-aware
- Enjoying the relationship

- Being coached
- Being encouraged
- Learning how the organisation works
- Fostering the mentoring relationship
- Sharing critical knowledge
- Developing greater self-confidence
- Being assisted in developing their careers

# THE MENTORING PROCESS

## MENTEES' EXPECTATIONS

New and inexperienced mentees may have **unrealistic** expectations.
For instance, they may expect to:

- Be managed and adopt a passive role
- Be given career opportunities on a plate
- Be given answers to problems
- Be told what to do
- Have an easy ride
- Receive favours
- End mentoring when the immediate problem or issue appears to be sorted out
- Gossip and whinge

An inexperienced mentee may need a lot of support and gentle challenge if they have such ideas!

# FROM THE FRONT LINE

"Mentoring is about learning, and one thing I learned is how to be a mentee. In a way, this is the greatest benefit of all. Now it's as if I can mentor myself, and this includes seeking help when I need it. I'm also beginning to think I would like to mentor someone else."

A mentee

# WHAT MENTEES NEED

A systematic approach, such as the 3-Stage Model, increases the effectiveness of mentoring. At the same time, mentees look for different things, such as:

- A sounding-board and listener
- A giver of encouragement
- A critical friend
- A source of emotional support
- A confidant
- A source of knowledge

# THE MENTORING PROCESS

## AREAS FOR DISCUSSION

Mentees and mentors talk about:

- The mentee's work-related issues
- The mentor's work-related issues
- Career development
- Leadership issues
- Learning and development
- Problems and challenges
- Issues with 'difficult' people
- Performance issues
- Time management
- Personal issues
- Domestic issues

# WORKING TOGETHER

# THE FIRST MEETING

> *"I was assigned a mentor when I took up a new post and I very quickly realised how helpful he would be to me. He was approachable, enthusiastic and very capable, and I did not feel silly asking basic questions."*

An inexperienced mentee

# THE FIRST MEETING

## KEY ISSUES

**Preparation.** It is helpful to have an agenda for each meeting. Reflect on the nature of mentoring, the process as well as the outcomes. Think about your commitment to using mentoring well and giving it adequate time.

**Getting to know each other.** Give this enough time; it is the basis of trust and working well together. Share experiences from your pasts.

**Time.** Your relationship will change over time. Many mentees and mentors notice that discussion topics widen and deepen.

**Difficulties.** Sometimes things may go wrong. Nothing can replace honest and open discussion about the relationship. Try to let others know about the existence of your mentoring relationship to avoid any misunderstanding or resentment. Keep the relationship under review.

**Ground rules.** Establish ground rules. These will include:
- **Confidentiality:** this is essential. Agree between yourselves the boundaries of the relationship
- **Time commitment:** how much and how often?
- **Location:** where are you going to meet?
- **Recording meetings:** will you record your meeting and, if so, how (a diary or log)?

(77)

# RELATIONSHIP DIMENSIONS

The following may help establish the ground rules and act as a framework for reviewing the relationship.

| OPEN | CLOSED |

| PUBLIC | PRIVATE |

| FORMAL | INFORMAL |

| ACTIVE | PASSIVE |

| STABLE | UNSTABLE |

# RELATIONSHIP DIMENSIONS

The **open**/**closed** dimension is about the content.  What kind of things will be talked about?  This is up for discussion.  If it is **open**, then anything is on the agenda.  If it is **closed**, the discussion may be focused on specific issues.

The **public**/**private** dimension is about who knows mentoring is going on.  If the mentoring is in an organisation, keeping it **private** may lead to speculation about its purpose and nature.  Making it **public** is good for mentoring and good for the relationship in the organisational context.

The **formal**/**informal** dimension is about the administration and management of the relationship.  In a **formal** arrangement, the mentoring pair may agree meetings in advance, take notes, time limit the discussion, agree to meet in a regular venue at regular intervals.  If it is **informal** they will meet on an 'as required basis' and generally work on a 'go with the flow' basis.

# RELATIONSHIP DIMENSIONS

The **active/passive** dimension is about activity.  Who does what in the relationship?
The mentee is the more **active** in the relationship as he or she is the one undergoing
change and carrying out action plans.  The mentor may also agree to take some actions,
such as gathering information for the mentee, and may indeed, at times, ask the mentee
for a meeting.  If both feel the mentoring is **passive**, if not much is happening, it is
probably time to review the mentoring relationship.

The **stable/unstable** dimension is about trust and consistency. It is about sticking to the
ground rules while being prepared to jointly review them.  It is about sticking to the
meeting schedule and not changing it (particularly at the last minute).  It is about
developing momentum to the mentoring  process (by using the 3-Stage Model, for
example) and maintaining it.

# MAINTAINING THE PARTNERSHIP

Like any worthwhile relationship, mentoring relationships have natural life cycles:

- Searching
- Getting together
- Getting to know each other
- Developing trust
- Working together
- Ending the relationship
- Parting or developing a different kind of relationship, eg friendship

# MAINTAINING THE PARTNERSHIP

## MENTOR'S ROLE

To keep the partnership going through the life cycle it is important to consider your attitude as a mentor and the climate you help to create with your mentee.

The climate needs to be relaxed, open and encouraging. This can be influenced by a number of things:

- The relationship you have previously established:
    - How well do you know the person?
    - How much trust is there already?
    - What do you have in common?
    - What are your differences?
- The level of priority you give to mentoring:
    - Is it important to you?
    - Are you aware of how beneficial mentoring can be to you, the mentee and your organisation?
    - How serious are you about the business of helping others?

# MAINTAINING THE PARTNERSHIP

## MENTOR'S ROLE (Cont'd)

The climate can also be helped by:

- Sitting in a relaxed manner in comfortable surroundings

- Privacy

- Asking open questions and listening carefully to the responses

- Being prepared, on occasion, to talk openly about yourself

- Reviewing the ground rules and the nature of the relationship

- Having a cup of tea, or coffee, or spring water!

# MAINTAINING THE PARTNERSHIP

## MENTEE'S ROLE

As a **mentee** your attitude towards your mentor will contribute to the climate. Be prepared to:

- Talk about yourself
- Listen and ask questions
- View this first meeting as a social event aimed at building a longer-term learning relationship
- Establish the agenda and the ground rules
- Review the relationship periodically and when necessary

# MENTORING BY EMAIL & PHONE

A face-to-face meeting is the usual setting for mentoring.  However, mentoring can also take place by email and/or by telephone.  This extends the opportunities for mentoring when regular face-to-face meetings are not feasible, as an alternative or additional way to communicate and work together.

Because of its *distance*, e-mentoring has the potential to help the mentee to discuss issues openly and may help overcome any embarrassment or inhibition, paving the way for serious dialogue and constructive change.  It also offers scope for mentor and mentee to reflect on the content of their exchanges.

WORKING TOGETHER

# MENTORING AT A DISTANCE
## GOOD PRACTICE GUIDELINES

- If possible, meet face-to-face at least once before the 'distance' mentoring begins (three meetings is optimal). If this is not possible, follow the principles of the first meeting described earlier (page 77), and allow time for a good working relationship to develop

- The ground rules and boundaries that underpin face-to-face mentoring apply with equal importance at a distance

- Agree timescales for checking and exchanging emails and/or calls (whether daily/once a week/fortnightly). This will vary at different stages of the mentoring relationship

- Agree response times to emails/phone messages – within 24 or 48 hours, for example

- Be ready to seek clarification to avoid misunderstandings and jumping to conclusions

# FROM THE FRONT LINE

> *"I very quickly realised that this particular mentor was not for me. So we discussed it and agreed to end it. There was no loss of face on anyone's part. We tried, and it didn't work out. That's fine. Think what it would have been like if we had carried on regardless!"*
>
> A mentee

# HOW TO END IT

This is the only certain event in the relationship!  The end may happen when the mentee has reached a stage when he/she no longer feels the need for regular contact.  The mentee is confident and able to move on.  It is important to consider how it will end.  If the relationship has been successful, there will be cause for celebration *and* a sense of loss.  Attend to both.

You may agree to meet socially or less frequently or simply call a halt.

Look back and review your mentoring relationship and what you value about it:

- What were your original goals and were they achieved?
- Did they change, did you discover new goals/aspirations?
- What problems did you have and how did you resolve them?
- Would you seek a mentoring relationship again?
- What have you valued in mentoring, in the process as well as the outcomes?

# FROM THE FRONT LINE

> *"When this mentoring relationship comes to an end, you will want to move on. There will be other people who come along in your life who will become your mentor."*
>
> A mentee in financial services

NOTES

# MENTORING SCHEMES

# KEY FACTORS

Much can be done to promote mentoring in an organisation.  Two factors are key:

> The success of any organisational mentoring scheme
> is dependent to a significant degree
> on the visible participation
> of senior managers as mentors and mentees.

And

> Successful mentoring schemes
> usually start small and grow gradually,
> stimulated by enthusiasm and positive example, and
> organisational support.

MENTORING SCHEMES

# SCHEME DESIGN

If you have responsibility for designing and promoting a mentoring scheme, the following guidance will be useful.

**Establish the purpose of the scheme**
Who is mentoring aimed at?
What is it for?
What are the expectations of the scheme?

**Identify factors that will support or hinder mentoring in the organisation**
What mentoring is already taking place?
Identify people who are enthusiastic about mentoring
Identify people who are positive about learning and development
Will the scheme have top management support?
Will senior management participate?
Are people willing/unwilling to give their time?
Are people too busy?
Is learning and development valued throughout the organisation?

# SCHEME DESIGN

| | |
|---|---|
| **Develop an implementation plan to address the following** | Providing support for mentors and mentees<br>Responding to queries, apprehensions and and uncertainties<br>Identifying enthusiastic people to be 'pioneer' mentors and mentees in the organisation |
| **Evaluate** | See pages 103 onwards for advice on evaluation |

# DEVELOPING & PROMOTING THE SCHEME

- Start from where there is interest
- Train and support these people in mentoring skills
- Invite mentors and mentees to share their experiences through in-house newsletters, and other channels of organisational communication
- Have regular updates of progress in the scheme
- Publicise the mentoring partnerships
- Make mentoring part of training programmes
- Offer mentoring during and following a training programme
- Regularly review the scheme
- Don't expect that mentoring will solve all organisational problems

MENTORING SCHEMES

# FROM THE FRONT LINE

> *"Mentoring schemes work best when they are not introduced as the new initiative that will solve organisational problems.  Start small with positive volunteers and then watch it spread by word of mouth."*
>
> Experienced Scheme Co-ordinator

# MATCHING

- Sometimes two people will match themselves as mentor and mentee without any outside help. Usually, bringing mentor and mentee together is facilitated

- Some organisations publish lists of 'approved' mentors who are often volunteers with some training and who may provide a short pen-picture of themselves to help mentees make their choice

- Other organisations simply put people together. In this case there ought to be a logical system, clearly understood by both parties

- The 'dating agency' approach is sometimes used. Personal profiles and information, and sometimes standard tests and assessments are used to match people

- Matching should be done sensitively and with care. Mentoring is like any other human relationship - it needs time to develop

- Always suggest that people contract for three initial meetings and then review. If they are happy, they continue, if they are not they can have a 'no fault divorce'!

## MENTORING SCHEMES

# MATCHING

Commonly used criteria for matching:

- Culture/nationality
- Gender/sex
- Experience/background
- Personality characteristics
- Knowledge wanted/offered
- General 'wants'/'offers' approach
- Profiling eg Myers Briggs, emotional intelligence, learning styles
- Location/geography
- Tenure
- Common interests

# MATCHING

Scheme co-ordinators will consider the following questions about matching:

- Will you match for similarity or difference?
  (Each has its merits)

- Will you allow, or wait for, people to
  sort out their own arrangements?

- Will you actively match or just
  give guidance?

# ROLE OF SCHEME CO-ORDINATOR

The scheme co-ordinator will have a special role to play in helping sort out any difficulties. It is important to be aware of the kinds of difficulties that can arise.

**What can go wrong?**

**In the relationship:**

- Role confusion
- No boundaries set
- Lack of effort
- Personality clash
- Lack of commitment
- Lack of trust
- Insufficient time input
- Lack of training of mentors and mentees
- Lack of support for mentors
- Mentor's or organisation's agenda rather than mentee's

**In the scheme:**

- Lack of voluntarism and choice
- Confusion about what mentoring is
- Confusion about the purpose of mentoring
- Organisational culture
- Wrong measurement, wrong expectations
- Insufficient time input
- No senior management buy in
- Management style
- Power/control obsession
- No support for mentors

# FROM THE FRONT LINE

> *"Introducing mentoring did create interest but it also raised concerns. We approached the concerns in the 'mentoring way' by listening to them and trying to adjust the scheme design to match. The results were much better than we dared to hope for!"*
>
> Training Manager, large private sector business

MENTORING SCHEMES

# CONDITIONS FOR SUCCESS

The main conditions for success of a mentoring scheme are:

- Voluntary participation and choice
- Clear recruitment strategy
- Training of mentors and mentees
- Ongoing support for mentors and mentees if they require it
- A clear and transparent matching policy
- Establishing ground rules
- Ongoing review
- Working with the mentee's agenda
- Accepting mentoring as legitimate work

# EVALUATION

Systematic evaluation of a mentoring scheme will help to:

- Demonstrate the effectiveness of the scheme
- Develop the scheme
- Provide evidence to support it
- Give feedback about practice
- Identify any difficulties in the scheme and lead on to solutions

Evaluation is best started at the beginning of the scheme rather than at the end.
This is so that any problems may be identified and resolved as the scheme progresses.
Far better to deal with issues as they arise than wait for an 'end point' evaluation to learn that things have gone wrong!

# EVALUATION

'Not everything that counts can be counted. And, not everything that can be counted counts.'
Einstein

In relation to mentoring, Einstein was right! When evaluating mentoring, there are things that can be counted that are of interest but have limited impact on the effectiveness of mentoring. Also, there are things that count that can't be directly counted but are strongly associated with the benefits of mentoring activity.

MENTORING SCHEMES

# EVALUATION

**Things that can be counted and are of interest:**

- Numbers of people participating
- Duration of relationships
- Numbers of people who have received training and support
- The cost of training and support

# EVALUATION

**Things that count but can't be directly counted:**

- Successful and productive relationships
- Increased performance, sales figures, better bottom-line and appraisal ratings
- Reduced crime and re-offending in young offenders' schemes (although some claim this can be counted)
- Improved numbers in employment (in employment related schemes: again some claim that this can be directly counted)
- Improved staff retention rates, increased job satisfaction and confidence
- Improved motivation and morale, reduced conflict
- Better knowledge and skills transfer, improved awareness of self and others
- Leadership development and succession planning
- Increased opportunity, managing change and HR policy implementation

MENTORING SCHEMES

# FROM THE FRONT LINE

> "We have found that mentoring is good for the mentee,
> good for the mentor and good for the organisation."
>
> Learning and Development Manager

## MENTORING SCHEMES

# EVALUATION

### What can be evaluated?

- The relationships
- Relationship outcomes
- Scheme processes
- Scheme outcomes
- Line management opinion
- Other stakeholders' views including customers

### Useful evaluation points

- At scheme planning stage
- At selection and training stage
- After the first few meetings
- As the relationships progress
- At the end of the relationship
- At the end of the scheme

# MENTOR SUPPORT

Mentoring skills take a while to acquire and on-going support for mentors helps their skills to develop.

Support can take three different forms:

- Mentoring supervision
- Mentor support group
- Learning set

# MENTORING SUPERVISION

Supervision is a quality control process to help the mentor:

- Develop confidence and skills as a mentor
- Demonstrate skill and knowledge
- Provide a different angle on an issue
- Increase self understanding, as a result of mentoring
- Celebrate success as a mentor
- Identify and address any difficulties, frustrations and blind spots in being a mentor
- Prevent personal burn out

# MENTORING SUPERVISION

The supervisor's role is to:

✔ Help debrief the mentor
✔ Discuss and work on skills and process issues

The supervisor's role is NOT to:

✘ Discuss the content of the mentor's discussions with their mentee

The supervisor could be another mentor. The frequency of supervision meetings will depend on the number of mentees the mentor has. Approximately every three months is a good benchmark.

# MENTOR SUPPORT GROUP

Some organisations support their mentor development through regular mentor meetings. Here the participants discuss skills and process issues collectively. In some organisations mentees attend these meetings.

It is a good idea to have more experienced mentors running these meetings.

MENTORING SCHEMES

# LEARNING SET

Another approach to mentor support is through learning set methodology. It often takes about 3-4 months of regular mentoring meetings for a new mentor to develop their skills and experience of the 3-stage process.

During this time, new mentors can get a lot of support, focused on their practice, from learning sets.

Learning sets normally consist of about six members with one person being the facilitator.

Each participant has a time slot during which members of the set focus on the participant's mentoring practice issue.

The set will offer opinion, advice, challenge and support to each other. This is a bit like group mentoring in fact!

# STANDARDS & QUALIFICATIONS

Two professional organisations have established standards for mentoring and coaching practice.

The European Mentoring and Coaching Council (EMCC) has established its standards through research among the mentoring and coaching community. The EMCC also has a kitemarking process to accredit educational and training courses in mentoring and coaching. If you are looking for courses on mentoring and coaching, it is advisable to seek EMCC kitemarked programmes to ensure they meet suitable standards.

The Chartered Institute of Personnel and Development (CIPD) are also developing standards of mentoring and coaching practice.

There is a range of universities now offering courses at Post Graduate Certificate, Post Graduate Diploma and Masters level. The two main providers in Mentoring are Sheffield Hallam University and Oxford Brookes.

The CIPD and the Open College have NVQ level programmes.

# ETHICS

Mentoring raises ethical questions.  It is important that mentoring is a positive experience for the participants.  Within schemes it is a good idea to establish ethical guidelines.

The following is based on the EMCC's ethical statement:

> Mentoring activity acknowledges the dignity of all participants.  Mentors and mentees respect diversity and promote equal opportunities.  It is the primary responsibility of the mentor to provide the best possible service to the mentee and to act in such a way as to cause no harm to the mentee or the host organisation.  Both the mentor and mentee are committed to functioning from a position of dignity, autonomy and personal responsibility.

# TIPS FOR MENTORS

1. Maintain regular contact.
2. Always be honest.
3. Avoid being judgemental.
4. Recognise that you have your own need for support. A mentor may need a mentor as well!
5. Don't expect to have all the answers.
6. Help your mentee access resources and further support.
7. Be clear about expectations and boundaries.
8. Stand back from the issues your mentee raises but work together on them.
9. Respect confidentiality.
10. If the relationship falters - hang on in there!

# MENTORING SCHEMES

# TIPS FOR MENTEES

1. Accept challenge willingly.
2. Share with your mentor how you feel about the way the relationship is working.
3. Maintain a positive view of yourself.
4. Be active in your own development.
5. Have faith and trust in your mentor.
6. Be willing to discuss issues openly.
7. Take a few risks in order to progress.
8. Think about other ways to develop yourself outside of your mentoring relationship.
9. Don't expect too much of your mentor.
10. Talk about the end of your relationship when the time comes.

# FROM THE FRONT LINE

> *"It was my mentor who convinced me that I was good enough, so that I could convince the senior managers of my readiness for promotion."*
>
> A mentee

# ISSUES & QUESTIONS

# MENTOR PROFILE

### Who should be a mentor?

Anyone who is interested. It may be a manager or a peer. A mentor needs to be somebody that a mentee can trust. A mentor is often, but not always, older than the mentee. A mentor may also have experience greater than, or different from, the mentee's. A mentor is someone who recognises their own need for help and support.

### What about potential conflict between the line manager and the mentor?

Ideally, your mentor should not be your line manager. There is some scope for confusion of roles. Many managers see that their role includes mentoring. However, most mentees value a degree of separation between the roles.

# MENTORING IN PRACTICE

### How much time is involved?

This will vary depending on the mentee's needs.  Average time in many organisations is 2-3 hours per month.

### What about bad mentoring?

The quality of mentoring depends in part upon circumstances and the environment. If the relationship does not work, be honest about it and either bring it to a close or try to resolve the differences.  Mentor training and ongoing support may help here.

### How many mentors/mentees can I have?

It is possible to have more than one mentor. Each mentor offers something different to the mentee, most often in areas of knowledge and technical expertise. Mentors may have more than one mentee.  It is really a question of how much time is available.

# MENTORING IN PRACTICE

### Who gets credit for mentoring?

Credit is perhaps the wrong word. Mentoring is a satisfying and productive activity for the participants and the organisation. Some organisations suggest that mentoring becomes part of an individual's Personal Development Plan.

### What is the scope of mentoring?

The scope is as broad as one would want it to be. Mentoring is primarily about learning and development. Mentoring is present when there are changes and transitions to go through at work and in individual lives. A mentor recognises the links between the personal and the professional aspects of a person's life and, through the mentoring process, can help to harmonise and, when necessary, reconcile the two.

### What about confidentiality?

Confidentiality is crucial. Secrecy is inappropriate. Everything in the mentoring relationship should be done by agreement.

# IMPROVING YOUR MENTORING SKILLS

### Do I need training?

It is a good idea for both mentors and mentees to consider doing some training in mentoring. This will help you to:

- Understand what is involved
- Understand how to get started
- Improve your confidence and commitment to mentoring
- Improve your mentoring skills
- Seek a mentor for yourself

### How do I improve as a mentor?

One way is to find a mentor for yourself. Another is to become part of a mentor support network with other mentors in your organisation. Further training and additional background reading (see page 125) are other options.

# MENTORING IN CONTEXT

### Should mentor and mentee be from the same ethnic/gender backgrounds?

In some situations this is very important. In general, the key to success is having a mentor who is able to listen, can be empathic towards the mentee and is committed to the mentee's welfare and the mentoring relationship. Regular review of the relationship is the most important element.

### Can mentoring solve all problems in the work place?

No! Mentoring is helpful in times of change, when someone starts a job or new project. Mentoring complements other development and training activities.

## FURTHER INFORMATION

**Books**

**_'Mentoring in Action'_**
(2nd edition) Megginson, D. et.al. (2005), Kogan Page

**_'Everyone Needs a Mentor'_**
(4th edition) Clutterbuck, D (2004), CIPD, London

**_'The Situational Mentor'_**
Clutterbuck, D and Lane, G (2004), Gower, Aldershot

**_'Mentoring and Diversity: An international perspective'_**
Clutterbuck, D and Ragins, BR (2002) Butterworth–Heinemann, Oxford

**_'Mentoring for Social Inclusion: A critical approach to nurturing mentor relationships'_**
Colley, H (2003) Routledge Falmer, London

**_'Techniques for Coaching and Mentoring'_**
Megginson, D and Clutterbuck, D (2005), Elsevier Butterworth-Heinemann, Oxford

| **Videos for Business** | **Videos for Community and Schools** |
|---|---|
| **_'Mentoring for Business Excellence'_** | **_'Peer Mentoring'_** |
| **_'Mentoring Conversations'_** | **_'New Chances, New Horizons'_** |
| **_'Mentoring the Dream'_** | **_'Learning Mentors'_** |

All videos available from: www.greenwood-partnership.com

# SOURCES OF INFORMATION

**The Coaching and Mentoring Research Unit at Sheffield Hallam University** is the leading centre in Europe for mentoring research, consultancy and education. Tel: 0114 225 3819 Web: http://www.shu.ac.uk/research/ciod/3/index.html Email:r.garvey@shu.ac.uk

**The Greenwood Partnership** is involved in all facets of mentoring from designing schemes, training mentors, research, evaluation and the design of paper based, video and CD-Rom learning materials. The Greenwood Partnership, 67 Prospect Road, St Albans AL1 2AU, Tel: 07957 380157 Email: kim@greenwood-partnership.com Web:www.greenwood-partnership.com

**The National Mentoring and Befriending Network** exists to promote mentoring in education and the community. There is a regional network, newsletter and a range of publications. Web: www.mandbf.org.uk

**The European Mentoring and Coaching Council** is the main European professional body for mentoring and coaching. It maintains a library and online database on mentoring, organises the annual European Mentoring and Coaching Conference, promotes research into mentoring and publishes a biannual online journal (The International Journal of Mentoring and Coaching) and publishes a quarterly newsletter. The council can be contacted via their website www.emccouncil.org

A helpful website on **e-mentoring** can be found at www.e-mentoringeurope.com See also Mentoring in Action by Megginson D. et.al (2005), Kogan Page, for case studies on e-mentoring.

## About the Authors

This book was produced collaboratively by Bob Garvey of the Coaching and Mentoring Research Unit at Sheffield Hallam University, Geof Alred, Honorary Fellow at Durham University, and Richard Smith, professor at Durham University.

**Geof Alred, MA, Ph.D, Adv. Dip. Counselling, CPsychol, CSci**.
Geof has wide experience of education, training and professional development.
He is a counsellor and counsellor trainer. His consultancy and research interests include mentoring and learning in organisations.

**Professor Bob Garvey, Cert.Ed., MA., Ph.D**
Bob is leader of the Coaching and Mentoring Research Unit at Sheffield Hallam University. He works with individuals and organisations helping them to understand and apply mentoring in the work place. He has published extensively on the subject of mentoring in both academic and professional journals. Bob is both a mentor and a mentee.

**Professor Richard Smith, BA, M.Ed.**
Richard has wide experience of training, mentoring and promoting 'learning organisations', both in the UK and beyond. He has a particular interest in ethical issues, as well as in education in all its dimensions.

# ORDER FORM

## Your details

Name _____

Position _____

Company _____

Address _____

_____

_____

Telephone _____

Fax _____

E-mail _____

VAT No. (EC companies) _____

Your Order Ref _____

## Please send me:

No. copies

The <u>Mentoring</u> Pocketbook ☐

The _____ Pocketbook ☐

The _____ Pocketbook ☐

The _____ Pocketbook ☐

### Order by Post

**MANAGEMENT POCKETBOOKS LTD**

LAUREL HOUSE, STATION APPROACH,
ALRESFORD, HAMPSHIRE SO24 9JH UK

### Order by Phone, Fax or Internet

Telephone: +44 (0)1962 735573
Facsimile: +44 (0)1962 733637
E-mail: sales@pocketbook.co.uk
Web: www.pocketbook.co.uk

*Customers in USA should contact:*
**Management Pocketbooks**
2427 Bond Street, University Park, IL 60466
Telephone: 866 620 6944   Facsimile: 708 534 7803
E-mail: mp.orders@ware-pak.com
Web: www.managementpocketbooks.com